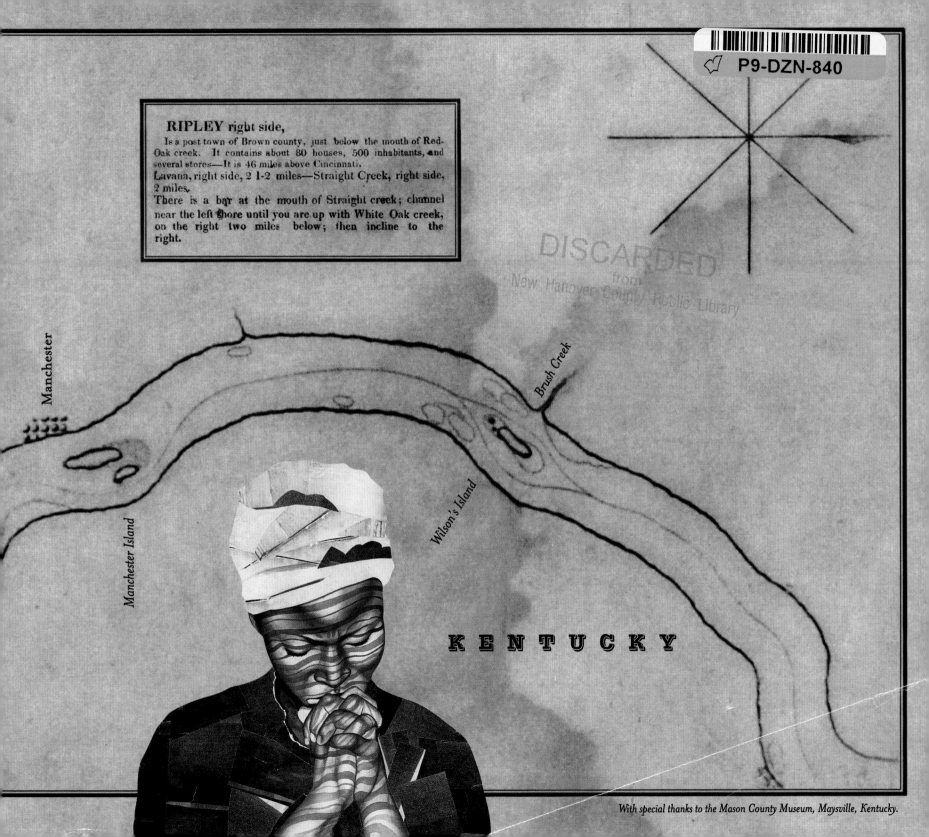

RIPLEY right side,

Is a post town of Brown county, just below the mouth of Red-Oak creek. It contains about 80 houses, 500 inhabitants, and several stores—It is 46 miles above Cincinnati.
Lavana, right side, 2 1-2 miles—Straight Creek, right side, 2 miles.
There is a bar at the mouth of Straight creek; channel near the left shore until you are up with White Oak creek, on the right two miles below; then incline to the right.

Manchester

Brush Creek

Manchester Island

Wilson's Island

KENTUCKY

With special thanks to the Mason County Museum, Maysville, Kentucky.

FREEDOM RIVER

—o—

DOREEN RAPPAPORT

—o—

PICTURES BY

BRYAN COLLIER

JUMP AT THE SUN

HYPERION BOOKS FOR CHILDREN · NEW YORK

To my dear friend William Greenidge—D.R.

Thank God for the power of prayer and for all the members
of the Emmanuel Baptist Church, Brooklyn, New York—B.C.

AUTHOR'S NOTE

When I first read about John Parker, I was stunned by his courage and determination. At the time of the event in this story, he was a prosperous businessman with a family he loved. But John Parker was not just content with his freedom and good fortune. He felt he had a higher responsibility than to just take care of himself and his immediate family. He saw himself as a protector for people still enslaved. Over and over again he risked his freedom to help others. Getting caught would have meant imprisonment or death.

John Parker reminded me of other freedom fighters such as Harriet Tubman and Sojourner Truth. His story is one of many stories being discovered that enrich our understanding of American history. I am privileged and proud to have written about him.

ILLUSTRATOR'S NOTE

For me, John Parker's story of courage and determination is also a story about the power of prayer. I believe in praying in our ordinary, day-to-day lives, as well as in times of great trouble. When I was growing up, I knew many old folks who really knew how to pray, and that's something you pass on, one generation to the next. I also believe in guardians who protect us, just as my African ancestors believed that guardians watched over them, even when they were enslaved in the New World. These guardians take many forms. When I was a child, I knew many black parents and grandparents who were poor and unable to read, but they were so determined that their children get educated, and they sacrificed much to do so. I wanted children to know about these protectors, so I incorporated them into my illustrations. At different places in the text, you will see people who are not part of the main illustration: these are the ancestors or protectors of Sarah and Isaac and their child. Their faces are modeled on the deacon, the deaconess, and the pastor of my church—individuals who provide me with spiritual guidance. The wavy lines across their faces represent the river, for the river is the key to freedom.

Text copyright © 2000 by Doreen Rappaport   Illustrations copyright © 2000 by Bryan Collier

All rights reserved. No part of this book may be reproduced or transmitted in any form or by any means, electronic or mechanical, including photocopying, recording, or by any information storage and retrieval system, without written permission from the publisher.
For information address Hyperion Books for Children, 114 Fifth Avenue, New York, New York 10011-5690.
Designed by Christine Kettner   3 5 7 9 10 8 6 4

Visit www.jumpatthesun.com

LIBRARY OF CONGRESS CATALOGING-IN-PUBLICATION DATA
Rappaport, Doreen. Freedom River / Doreen Rappaport : illustrated by Bryan Collier. —1st ed. p. cm.
Includes bibliographical references and index. Summary: Describes an incident in the life of John Parker, an ex-slave who became a successful businessman in Ripley, Ohio, and who repeatedly risked his life to help other slaves escape to freedom. ISBN 0-7868-0350-9.—ISBN 0-7868-1229-X (pbk.).—ISBN 0-7868-2291-0 (lib. bdg.).
Parker, John P., 1827–1900—Juvenile literature. 2. Underground railroad—Juvenile literature. 3. Afro-American abolitionists Biography—Juvenile literature. 4. Free Afro-Americans Biography—Juvenile literature. 5. Slaves—United States Biography Juvenile literature. 6. Ripley (Ohio) Biography Juvenile literature. [1. Parker, Johnm P., 1827–1900. 2. Underground railroad. 3. Abolitionists. 4. Slavery. 5. Afro-Americans Biography.] I. Collier, Bryan, ill. II. Title. E450.R23 2000 973.7'115—dc21 [B] 99-33438

BEFORE THE CIVIL WAR, Kentucky was a slave state and Ohio a free state. In the 1800s the Ohio River was less than 1,000 feet wide at Ripley, Ohio. Runaway slaves from Kentucky followed the Maysville Road to thè river and then swam or were rowed across it to freedom. Sympathetic whites and blacks in Ripley hid the fugitives and then transported them farther north.

John Parker was a successful businessperson and one of Ripley's most active conductors on the Underground Railroad. He had been born a slave and earned enough money to buy his freedom. But he never forgot the pain of being taken from his mother's loving arms when he was eight years old. This is a true story of one of his journeys into Kentucky to help an African American family escape to freedom.

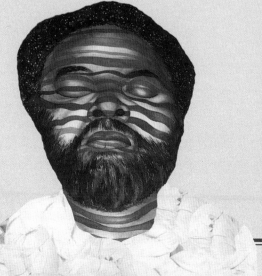

Listen. Listen.

"**I** heard last night someone helped a slave woman cross the river," said one of the workers at John Parker's foundry.

John Parker couldn't take credit for this escape, but it pleased him enormously to hear about it.

"Maybe Mr. Parker helped them escape," said Jim Shrofe, an iron molder. "My father says he's helped hundreds." Jim raised his voice. "I dare him to cross the river and try to steal my father's slaves," taunted Jim. "If he does, my father will set the dogs on him and rip him to shreds."

John knew if he crossed the river, he might end up dead. There was a $1,000 reward for him, dead or alive, in Kentucky. But he couldn't let that stop him. Slavery was too evil. He had to keep helping others, no matter what the risk.

A week later in November, when the moon was but a sliver, John rowed across the Ohio River to the Shrofe plantation.

Wait, wait.
Listen. Listen.

Only crickets and bullfrogs breaking the silence of the fall night. Suddenly, footsteps. Closer. Louder. The crescent moon illuminated a black man. John approached him and touched him.

"I have a boat waiting to row you 'cross the river to freedom," he whispered.

"I-I-I can't go," the man stammered. "I can't leave my wife and baby." Without warning, the man screamed and ran away.

Suddenly, a white man, swinging a club, charged at John. John ducked. The man dropped his weapon and grabbed John around the waist. Down, down, the man wrestled him to the ground and punched him in the face. John grabbed a handful of dirt and threw it into the man's eyes.

Run, run. Back to the river. Back to his skiff.

Row, row. Away from the slave state of Kentucky to the free state of Ohio.

December came and brought patches of ice on the river. In January, the river froze. Rowing across it was impossible now. Jim Shrofe continued to taunt John that he was too scared to go after his father's slaves. John didn't answer his taunts. He practiced being patient as he waited for spring.

In April, when the river thawed, he returned to the plantation, even more determined.

Wait, wait.
Listen, listen.

The moon shone on the man John had seen in November. John followed him into a cabin. "I've come back for you and your family."

"Leave Isaac an' me alone," said the man's wife, Sarah. "Since you came last fall, Master Shrofe watches our ev'ry move. He took my baby from me an' makes her sleep ev'ry night at the foot of his bed."

"Isaac, sneak into his room while he sleeps and take her," John urged.

"Too dangerous," said Isaac. "The master keeps a loaded pistol at his side an' swears he will kill her an' anyone who comes for her."

John shuddered at Shrofe's cruelty, for he knew the baby's parents loved her too much to leave her behind. He returned home, but he could not sleep that night. He felt responsible for Sarah being separated from her baby. He had to get this family to freedom.

The next night he rowed across the river again. He tied his skiff to a wooden post and untied the other boat there. He smiled as it drifted away.

"Get up, get up." John shook Isaac and Sarah from sleep.

"Go away. Leave us alone," Sarah begged.

"I know you are afraid, but trust me. I will get your child out of Shrofe's bedroom," John said.

"No, no. It will never work," Sarah said. "He will kill you an' my baby."

"It will work," John insisted. "Wait for me in the woods. If you hear gunshots, run back to your cabin." He took off his shoes.

"Isaac, hold these until I return."

John hurried to the main house. Into the pantry. Into the kitchen. There was no sign of the vicious guard dogs Jim Shrofe had threatened him with.

Into the hall. Ahead, light seeped from under the door of Shrofe's bedroom. John tiptoed toward it. Still no dogs. He held his breath. The Lord must be watching over me, he thought.

He gently pushed the door open.

On the far side of the room, a candle flickered. Shrofe and his wife were sleeping. A pistol rested next to the candle. John clutched the gun in his pocket. He listened for the breathing of Shrofe and his wife. It was regular and smooth. He relaxed a bit. He saw the baby sleeping at the foot of the bed. She was no more than five feet away, but she seemed unreachable.

Crawl, crawl. The floor creaked slightly as he inched toward the child. Three feet more. Shrofe tossed restlessly in his sleep. Two feet. One foot. John scooped up the baby and threw her pillow at the candle. The room went dark. The pistol clanked to the floor. Shrofe awakened with a start.

Run, run. Down the hall, to the kitchen, through the pantry, out the door. The baby started crying. There was no time to soothe her. John heard Shrofe's running feet and cursing mouth close behind.

Run, run. Down the road, to the water, to the skiff. Isaac and Sarah ran close at John's heels. Gunshots rang out in the air behind them.

John untied his boat. "Get in and lower your heads," he ordered. Sarah clutched her baby. More gunfire.

Faster, faster. John pulled the oars and ignored the flashes of gunfire from the Kentucky side.

When the oars hit the Ohio shore, John sighed. He had tempted fate and won. He hurried his passengers onto shore.

"Isaac, my shoes."

"I dropped them when I was running."

No time to worry now.

Run, run. To the safe house. In minutes, the family was hidden under straw in a wagon, to be driven farther north by the next conductor on the Underground Railroad.

John was barely home when there was a banging at his front door. He walked slowly downstairs. "Who is it?" he asked.

"Jim Shrofe."

John opened the door and pretended surprise. "Why are you here?"

Jim pushed John's shoes into his face. "To exchange your shoes for my father's slaves."

"I've never seen those shoes before, and I don't want them," said John indignantly. His tone turned gracious. "But you are welcome to come in and look for your missing slaves."

Jim gripped the shoes tightly in his hands and searched room after room. He banged closet doors, knocked on walls, pulled out drawers, and threw clothing on the floor. John did not care about the noise or the mess, for the longer Jim searched, the greater the head start for Sarah, Isaac, and their child.

Listen, listen.

"I heard someone rowed a slave family across the river last night," said one of John's workers.

John waited to hear what Jim Shrofe would say. He did not hear his voice. Jim had not reported to work this morning. He never returned to work for John Parker.

HISTORICAL NOTE

John Parker was born in 1827 in Norfolk, Virginia, to a slave mother and white father. When he was eight, he was sold to a doctor in Mobile, Alabama. The doctor's sons defied the slave laws and taught him to read and write. When John was twelve, he was apprenticed to a plasterer who beat him so badly that he ended up in a hospital. While recuperating, he escaped, but was captured in New Orleans.

He was next apprenticed to an iron molder. He mastered the work but was fired for fighting with his boss. His next job also resulted in dismissal. John was now sixteen years old. His owner decided to sell him, for he believed that John's defiant nature would continually get him into trouble.

John convinced one of his owner's clients to buy him and let him earn his freedom by repaying her from monies he would earn. He worked seven days a week. In eighteen months he earned $1,800, a huge sum then. He bought his freedom.

On May 12, 1848, he married Miranda Boulen. They settled in Ripley, Ohio. Ripley was a center of antislavery activity. The Ripley Abolition Society boasted over 300 members, black and white.

John became a successful and respected businessperson. He patented a tobacco press and manufactured it along with engines, reapers, mowers, and steel plows. At one time he employed more than twenty-five men, black and white. He and his wife raised eight children. But happiness and success never erased his painful years as a slave and the separation from his mother. Time and time again he risked his life to help slaves escape. Historians believe he might have helped as many as 900 African Americans.

John Parker died on January 30, 1900. His house on Front Street is now a museum.

To re-create this incident, I relied on *His Promised Land: The Autobiography of John Parker, Former Slave and Conductor*, published by W. W. Norton in 1997, and on documents provided by William R. Erwin, Jr., senior reference librarian, Duke University, and other first-person accounts by Parker, plus newspaper articles provided by Union Township Public Library in Ripley, Ohio. I took the liberty of filling in certain details that Parker did not provide, such as the names of the black family, and the month of this daring escape. I am grateful to Alison Gibson, librarian at the Union Township Public Library, for patiently answering my many questions. I thank Dr. Stuart Seely Sprague, Professor Emeritus of History, Morehead State University, who edited Parker's autobiography for publication, for reviewing my manuscript.

ADDITIONAL BOOKS AND WEBSITES:

Douglass, Frederick. *Escape from Slavery: The Boyhood of Frederick Douglass in His Own Words*. Edited and illustrated by Michael McCurdy. New York: Knopf, 1994.

Haskins, James. *Get on Board: The Story of the Underground Railroad*.
New York: Scholastic, 1993.

Rappaport, Doreen. *Escape from Slavery: Five Journeys to Freedom*. Illustrated by Charles Lilly. New York: HarperCollins, 1991.

Ringgold, Faith. *Aunt Harriet's Underground Railroad in the Sky*.
New York: Crown, 1992.

Winter, Jeanette. *Follow the Drinking Gourd*. New York: Knopf, 1988.

www.cr.nps.gov/nr/underground/oh2.htm
www.underground railroad.com
www.ripley.k12.oh.us/ripley/historicripley/parker.htm

Straight Creek

Lavana

Dover

← RIPLEY

Redeah Creek

Eagle Creek

Charleston

OHIO

Breck's Island

THE

WESTERN PILOT;

CONTAINING CHARTS OF THE OHIO RIVER

AND OF THE

MISSISSIPPI,

FROM THE MOUTH OF THE MISSOURI TO THE GULF OF MEXICO;

ACCOMPANIED WITH

DIRECTIONS FOR NAVIGATING THE SAME,

AND A

GAZETTEER:

OR DESCRIPTION OF THE TOWNS ON THEIR BANKS, TRIBUTARY STREAMS, ETC., ALSO, A VARIETY OF MATTER INTERESTING TO TRAVELERS, AND ALL CONCERNED IN THE NAVIGATION OF THOSE RIVERS; WITH A TABLE OF DISTANCES FROM TOWN TO TOWN ON ALL THE ABOVE RIVERS.

BY SAMUEL CUMMINGS.

CONTAINING THE POPULATION OF THE PRINCIPAL TOWNS ON THE RIVER IN 1846.

REVISED AND CORRECTED EVERY YEAR

BY CAPTS. CHARLES ROSS & JOHN KLINEFELTER,

CINCINNATI:
PUBLISHED BY GEORGE CONCLIN.
1847.

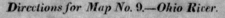

Directions for Map No. 9.—Ohio River.

MAYSVILLE.

MAYSVILLE, formerly called Limestone, stands on the Kentucky shore just below Limestone creek. It has a fine harbour for boats. It is situated on a narrow bottom between the high hills, which rise just behind it, and the Ohio. It has three streets, running parallel with the river; and four crossing them at right angles. The houses are about 500, and the inhabitants nearly 5000. It is the depot of the goods and merchandize intended to supply the eastern part of the State of Kentucky, which are imported from Philadelphia and the Eastern cities, and which are landed here, and distributed all over the State. The great road, leading from Lexington to Chillicothe, also crosses here. It is a very thriving, active town. Washington, the county town, and a wealthy village is situated 4 miles South-west from Maysville, and is surrounded by a fertile and populous country.